SAFE TRAVELS

An Essential Guide to Safely Journeying with Psilocybin.

By

Kelly Hanner

Table of Contents

Note from the Author

I am not a mycologist – someone who studies mushrooms. This book is not a definitive resource on all things psychedelic mushrooms, as it only skims the surface when it comes to providing information and education about mushrooms. Nor is it medical advice at all. It is up to you as the reader to do your due diligence to learn more about mushrooms and to discuss with your doctor if psilocybin is right for you. This book is not meant to diagnose nor am I ever suggesting you stop taking any medications without consulting your doctor and deriving a plan of action. As mentioned in later chapters, there are many realms related to psilocybin that are illegal, so please be mindful of this proceeding forward. I do not condone, endorse, or encourage doing anything illegal, tread lightly and understand that anything you do after reading this book is your own responsibility. This ebook also contains affiliate links.

Affiliate Disclosure
In compliance with the FTC guidelines, please assume the following about all links in this ebook:
Any/all of the links on this website are affiliate links of which Kelly Hanner, LLC receives a small commission from sales of certain items, but the price is the same for you.

Kelly Hanner LLC is a participant in the Amazon Services LLC Associates Program, an affiliate advertising program designed to provide a means for affiliates to earn advertising fees by advertising and linking to Amazon.com. Pages within this book may include affiliate links to Amazon and its affiliate sites on which the owner of this book will make a referral commission.

Introduction

We had just taken the psychedelic mushrooms about a half hour ago. I was a sophomore in high school sitting in my best friend's basement when they started to kick in. As we sat around the table, I looked out to a friend sitting across from me. His freckles jumped off his face and started dancing around before falling back into place. We took a dose big enough to produce visualizations, but not high enough to produce any massive life revelations. As our evening started to come to an end, I laid down in my girlfriend's bed. Looking up, I stared in amazement at the glow in the dark plastic stars that were fixated on her ceiling. They sparkled and shimmered just like, if not better, than the stars on a clear, dark night.

My first experience with mushrooms would forever stand out in my mind as a really incredible experience. Seeing the way that reality could morph before your very own eyes has a lasting impression – something you never forget. The set and setting (which we will get into with more detail later) for my first trip was ideal – a familiar place with people I was comfortable with.

Ignorant to proper psychedelic use, the next time I did mushrooms was late night at a house party.

As a high schooler, I had a lot of social anxiety, and wasn't necessarily one of the cool kids. Here I was, chock full of social anxiety on mushrooms at a house party filled with all the cool kids. This trip was what I would go on to describe as a "bad trip." With all of the different personalities, while on mushrooms I felt out of sorts. I laid in a hammock outside, looking up to the trees when I saw a T-Rex come down from the trees at me. It was a mixed bag of one weird experience after another until I finally realized I needed to retreat away from everyone. I found myself in a bedroom, with the Goofy Movie on. The trip went from bad to worse, as much to my horror, the characters in the movie all formed a huddle and started talking about me.

Being that I grew up in the Midwest, getting a hold of mushrooms wasn't an easy thing to do, it was in fact a rarity, so partaking in mushrooms was a treat and something that didn't happen much more after that. Getting into a serious relationship in my early 20's, my partner was dead set on never doing mushrooms and didn't want me to do them either, so it wasn't until I got out of that relationship after 9 years where I was finally able to reconnect with the fungi.

Reuniting with mushrooms after my breakup, has been something that has completely altered my life forever – in only the best way possible. More mature and more in touch with the idea of being more intentional with my actions, I started taking mushrooms often. I created ceremonies where I would set an intention for the experience and would take small doses of mushrooms to help me connect to a deeper part of myself that I had been cut off to for years.

Being that I was a bulimic in my early 20's and dealt with various forms of disordered eating all throughout my life, psilocybin mushrooms helped me in a way therapy never could. While most psychiatrists will say that eating disorders are rooted in an effort to gain control over one's life, my eating disorder also stemmed from having zero self-confidence or self-love. It was through my mushroom trips, that the fog that had settled over me was lifted. I could see through the conditioning that taught me I wasn't good enough unless I was slim and fit into what society thought was sexy. Through mindful dosing, I could see my true self – pure, beautiful, and that there wasn't a damn thing wrong with me.

Since having many breakthroughs on various doses of mushrooms, it's become my mission to spread the word and remove the stigma of psychedelic mushroom use. While I don't think mushrooms are for everyone, I can't help but wonder what mindful use of psychedelic mushrooms could do for the people who could successfully dose with them. Not only that, but what could getting mushrooms into the hands of people who really need them do to shift the world in a more positive, united direction?

I believe we're in the dawn of a psychedelic renaissance. This is a time in which for whatever, possibly divine, reason we have circled back around to using psychedelics to journey into our consciousness and pierce into the other realms behind the veil. Maybe this is Mother Nature calling us back to our origins, helping us to remove the wall we have put up between us and nature.

It's for this reason that I decided to write this e-book. There's a lot to learn about psychedelic mushrooms, and there's a lot that needs to be understood if one wants to get the most benefit from taking a journey. Mushrooms are hard to come by, so should you ever cross paths with them, it's important to be well prepared to ensure you're getting the most out of your experience. If you decide to do mushrooms, I hope that this e-book can be a guide to help you do them in a safe way that provides lasting, monumental change.

In this book, I'll cover everything from how to get mushrooms, dosing, how to set yourself up for an experience that could change your entire life, and so much more.

Safe Travels

Chapter 1:

Why Would You Take Mushrooms?

There are plenty of reasons to take mushrooms. Recreationally, when done with people you enjoy in a setting you're comfortable in, mushrooms can be a really great way to bond with others. Helping to reduce social anxiety and peel back social norms, psilocybin can help to produce so many joyous laughs that your face can hurt the next day and can produce tears of joy and immense gratitude for the people you're with.

More-so, many people today are intrigued by the idea that mushrooms can help them mentally, physically, emotionally, and spiritually. Many are also interested in how it could help them to end addictions and negative behaviors. With Silicon Valley spreading the word about how micro dosing, taking a small enough amount of mushrooms that you won't feel any psychedelic effects, can help increase productivity while reducing anxiety, stress, and mental chatter. Prestigious research university Johns Hopkins is leading the way by being a major modern institution that is giving mushrooms serious consideration. For example, Johns Hopkins "researchers report that a substantial majority of people suffering cancer-related anxiety or depression found considerable relief for up to six months from a single large dose of psilocybin — the active compound in hallucinogenic 'magic mushrooms."1

Paul Stammets, renowned mycologist and fungi researcher, mentions that Johns Hopkins clinical trials have shown that using mushrooms in a clinical setting can be very helpful for people dealing with cancer and other life threatening illnesses, while also helping people with OCD, smoking cessation, to be better citizens within their communities, and even veterans with PTSD In their retroactive studies, 14 months later, researchers interviewed research participants' employers, family members, and friends. Those interviewed said that there had been a change for the better in the study's participants- they were easier to get along with; more empathetic, sympathetic, helpful, and less angry. The medical evidence thus shows that these experiences can create lasting positive effects in people's lives.[2]

In an article published by the Guardian, they state that magic mushrooms may also help to "effectively 'reset' the activity of key brain circuits known to play a role in depression." The head of psychedelic research at Imperial College, Dr. Robin Carhart-Harris, who led the study on 20 patients with treatment-resistant depression, stated "We have

---

[1]

https://www.hopkinsmedicine.org/news/media/releases/hallucinogenic_drug_psilocybin_eases_existential_anxiety_in_people_with_life_threatening_cancer

[2] https://youtu.be/_MTFq3m2qeg

10

shown for the first time clear changes in brain activity in depressed people treated with psilocybin after failing to respond to conventional treatments."[3] Following treatment, patients reported that their depressive symptoms decreased – stating they had improved mood and relief from stress.

In regards to spiritual effects felt through psychedelics, there was an interesting double-blind study done in 1962 on 20 graduate degree divinity student volunteers, known as the "Good Friday Experiment." While almost all the members of the study who had received the psilocybin mushrooms experienced a profound religious experience, what's even more incredible is that in a follow up 25-years later, "all of the subjects given psilocybin, except for one, described their experience as having elements of 'a genuine mystical nature and characterized it as one of the high points of their spiritual life."[4]

It's been my own personal experience that mushrooms have helped me to connect to a higher consciousness much more than I ever did through the years of going to service. Growing up going to a Catholic grade school, I felt disconnected from the church services and the teachings of the church. Through using magic mushrooms, especially while outside in nature, I haven't ever felt more connected

[3] https://www.theguardian.com/science/2017/oct/13/magic-mushrooms-reboot-brain-in-depressed-people-study

[4] https: //en.wikipedia.org/wiki/Marsh_Chapel_Experiment

to a higher power. For me personally, that higher power is easiest to connect to when outside, away from all the distractions of the modern world and more in touch with Mother Nature.

Chapter 2:

Obtaining Mushrooms

Easily the question I get asked the most is "where can I get mushrooms?" That's not easy to answer because as of the start of 2020 mushrooms are federally illegal, and even classified as a Schedule 1 Drug, by the United States Controlled Substances Act. A Schedule 1 drug is classified as:

1. The drug or other substance has a high potential for abuse.
2. The drug or other substance has no currently accepted medical use in treatment in the United States.
3. There is a lack of accepted safety for use of the drug or other substance under medical supervision.

Except as specifically authorized, it is illegal for any person:

1. To manufacture, distribute, or dispense, or possess with intent to manufacture, distribute, or dispense, a controlled substance; or

2. To create, distribute, or dispense, or possess with intent to distribute or dispense, a counterfeit substance.[5]

The act of actually purchasing or wild foraging psilocybin mushrooms is illegal. Not only has that but our system believed that there's a high risk of abusing mushrooms and that there's no medical use for them either. From my own personal experience, I don't believe either to be true. When done intentionally, mushroom journeys can provide a lot to process and understand. My experience with mushrooms has never led to a 10 day mushroom bender, getting lost in the sauce on psychedelic mushrooms while I totally block out the rest of the world as I dive into a bottomless pit of physical and mental addiction to mushrooms. In fact, it's quite the opposite – when I do mushrooms, it is always coupled with a healthy dose of resignation as I know I'm going to be faced with a trip that will teach me a lot and provide me with a lot to process. In fact, each intentional journey I have ever been on feels like doing 10 years of intensive therapy in only a 4-8 hour trip.

Modern science is finally starting to catch onto the medical and therapeutic benefits of mushrooms that have been known by indigenous cultures the world over for centuries. Now that modern science is catching on, it's my hope that our judicial system and government will catch on soon as well.

––––––––––––––––––––––––––

[5] https:
//en.wikipedia.org/wiki/List_of_Schedule_I_drugs_%28US%29

That said, as of February 2020, Oakland and Santa Cruz, California as well as Denver, Colorado have decriminalized mushrooms while many other places in the US are looking to do the same.

Psilocybin-containing-mushrooms grow on every continent of the earth. Psychedelic mushrooms can be cultivated or are also known to grow out in the wild, most popularly known to grow on cow manure. Finding them can be possible depending on where one lives. Eating wild foraged mushrooms is something I don't risk as I'm not a mycologist (someone who studies fungi) and I don't want to make the mistake of eating the wrong mushroom and going out by poisoning myself. So it's for this reason that if I were trying to source mushrooms it might be good to find a mycologist or a seasoned forager who can show you what to look for. There are resources online to help ID mushrooms which include iNaturalist app, Facebook groups, or places like Shroomery.org – I just advise proceeding with great caution. One misidentification can easily land one in the hospital or even six feet under. But even so if you do manage to ID wild mushrooms properly, foraging psychedelic mushrooms is very illegal, so tread lightly.

There are other countries that allow the use of psychedelic mushrooms like Mexico, Jamaica, parts of South America, and the Netherlands. If one wants to maximize their experience and has the funds to do so, one could begin by researching reputable places or retreat centers in these countries that offer mushrooms.

There are some underground therapists who use psychedelics in supervised treatment. Finding them is tough, basically one has to "know somebody who knows somebody", and especially if one is living in a state where psychedelic drugs are frowned upon.

As I said before, science is starting to catch on about how therapeutic mushrooms actually are. With this new excitement surrounding mushroom research, there are plenty of research projects that you could apply for that could allow the opportunity to journey in a very controlled, safe setting.

In most cases, you need to network or know someone who knows someone. Most people will say, that when you're truly ready to do mushrooms, they'll find you… and that's normally how it truly works out.

Chapter 3:

Precautions

I wouldn't be doing my due-diligence if I didn't share the precautions to take if you're considering dosing with magic mushrooms. While in a perfect world, I believe everyone should experience mushrooms in an intentional way, there are some people who should exercise caution or not partake at all.

Michelle Janikian the author of Your Psilocybin Mushroom Companion6 shares that people who are disqualified from participating in mushroom clinical trials are those with "hypertension and other underlying heart conditions; history of psychosis or psychotic spectrum disorder like schizophrenia; bipolar disorder; other persistent severe mental illness; as well as a first-degree relative with any of these psychiatric conditions. Also, for the time being, pregnant people are also excluded."

It's important to do one's due diligence to look further into whether any drugs they may be taking or any conditions an individual may have that aren't listed here could have a negative interaction with dosing mushrooms. I highly recommend Michelle Janikian's book that I mentioned above for a more in-

---

[6] Find her book here: https: //amzn.to/3bt7Ew3

depth breakdown of the contraindications of taking mushrooms with certain medicines, other psychedelics or "drugs", and the conditions mentioned.

Chapter 4:

How to Set Up For a Good Trip

If you've ever spoken with an experienced psychonaut[7] then you've probably heard of "set and setting" before. Coined by OG psychonaut, psychologist, writer and psychedelic advocate Timothy Leary, "set" refers to one's mindset before journeying while "setting" refers to one's social and physical environment for the trip.

Set and setting are important because to simply go into a mushroom journey, or any psychedelic for that matter, without considering one's set and setting or putting any intentional thought into your experience could very easily lead you down the road of having a "bad" trip. While I don't necessarily believe there is such a thing as a bad trip, because I believe inside every trip there is some kind of lesson to be learned if we're totally open to it, it's always smart to do what one can to avoid having bad experiences that could have been

---

[7] A psychonaut is a person who spends time exploring the universe right inside their own head. Usually with drugs/yoga/meditation. This person is on a quest to discover the self, and usually can be considered "realists". https://www.urbandictionary.com/define.php?term=psychonaut

preventable with a little preparation and consideration. In my opinion, the only way to have a total bad trip is to forgo set and setting, not have a trip sitter if you're new to this, and to overdo your dose.

Let's further break down set and setting.

SET

One's mindset going into a journey is imperative to the whole experience. It's important to ensure you're in a good mindset before the experience. If you've been having a bout of depressive, suicidal, or anxious thoughts I encourage you to work through them before diving in. It's important to understand that mushrooms will often bring up what you've been avoiding. They have a really great way of magnifying what people ignore, and helping one to see things for how they really are. This can help to get beyond these thoughts or memories to help break old patterns. If the idea of really peeling back the layers of the onion to work through what's been bugging you is incredibly intimidating or you feel could be detrimental to your current mental state, perhaps revisit the idea of journeying when you're in a better place.

It's natural to have hesitations or experienced mushrooms more than I can count, I still have a bit of reluctance to take them (all because as I've mentioned before, I know what I'm in for and most of the time my intention is to do some shadow work, something that I know I need, but I know it'll also whoop my ass in all the right ways).

Something that helps with hesitations is to go into the journey with an intention. As "woo" as it may sound, a well thought out intention helps to clear the mind while placing your focus on other things than just worrying. It also can help to calm down any incessant overthinking kind of thought patterns. Keep your intention in mind before dosing, while ingesting, and loosely think back to it while deep in a journey or should you trail off into a negative thought loop. If any unpleasant thoughts come up, take a few deep breaths while reflecting on your intention. It also helps to write your intention out, so that should you be deep within a trip and can't recall it, you have it written down to come back to. That said, I also encourage to use your intention loosely – don't become so attached to your intention that should you diverge from what your intention is to other things, that you start thinking your journey is a waste –often times during a journey I feel you're given what you need, even if it strays away from your intended course.

One of my favorite ways to improve my mindset before a journey is to get out in nature. Mushrooms have a way of naturally connecting one to nature, so there's no real better way than to clear your mind outdoors. In Katy Bowman's book Move Your DNA, she shares the idea of "forest bathing," which is the act of taking in the "atmosphere of the trees." She shares how in Japan there's been heavy research done on forest bathing or shinrin-yoku which has shown that it can lower our stress hormone cortisol, blood pressure, pulse rate and also reduces cerebral activity. What a hell of a way to set the tone for your journey.

21

Getting out in nature doesn't need to be some huge feat either. Do what makes you happy – whether that be just sitting out on a park bench reading a book, taking your dogs for a walk, or finding a quiet area to do some breath work, gaze at the clouds, or take a few gentle stretches.

There are many other ways to relax to ensure you're going into your journey with a good mindset. Pick what works for you. Some things that have personally been great for me are listening to uplifting music, partaking in an activity that calms my nerves or makes me happy like coloring, practicing deep breathing or EFT (Emotional Freedom Technique), going to a sensory deprivation tank, getting a massage, doing yoga or stretching, getting in a good laugh or hanging out with a friend, or enjoying a nice bubble bath before the journey.

I also encourage you to do mushrooms on a day in which you're free from responsibilities, especially anything that might trigger a stress response out of you. Place your phone on airplane mode and clear your schedule for the day. Doing mushrooms on a day off from work is optimal. No one wants to bring the baggage of a stressful work day or commute home from work into their trip.

Something to take note of if you're a parent- if you have children, I cannot stress enough getting a babysitter for the day/night of your journey. A trip can last somewhere around 4-8 hours, the last thing you want to worry about while journeying is tending to your children. Not just that, but mushrooms can be a very introspective experience, the last thing I know I would want while journeying, is to be going through an epiphany of sorts, really working through baggage and get pulled out of it by needing to break up my kids from fighting, or have to tend to a scraped knee. So to be on the safe side, take the worry off from your shoulders by getting a babysitter.

SETTING

The setting of your journey is just as important as your mindset going into it. As mentioned, setting is your social and physical environment while journeying.

When I first dabbled with psychedelics, I did them where they were most accessible to me, which often was parties. Now that I am older and know not only of the kind of deep work that can be done with mushrooms but also the deep rabbit holes psilocybin can spiral you down into, I like keeping the people around me while journeying to a bare minimum.

As a more "experienced" (I use that loosely) psychonaut, my deepest dives that have provided the most insight and help have been solo trips. With a history of disordered eating patterns, it's during my solo trips that I am able to really uncover all of the different patterns and mindsets that have kept me a slave to unhealthy eating patterns. My biggest healing moments, coming from stripping down butt naked in front of a big mirror where I can appreciate myself for how I show up in the world physically.

23

Some people have apprehension towards looking in the mirror or doing mirror work while on mushrooms, but I welcome it as a way to develop more self-love.

That said, I wouldn't recommend solo journeying for everyone, especially people new to mushrooms. In fact, I would recommend a part of your setting to include a trip sitter. A trip sitter is someone you know and trust who has hopefully had experience themselves with mushrooms, or at the very least is someone who is open to them and willing to hold space for you during your journey. This person would have to be willing to set aside time to journey the entire length of the experience with you, while also respecting your boundaries and also being mindful of when you may need some TLC. These are things to discuss with your trip sitter ahead of time. In the rare chance that shit could go sideways or at the very least you need someone to actually hold space for you, it's best if your trip sitter, no matter their experience with mushrooms, is sober during your journey so they can be fully present with you. Michelle Janikian's book *Your Psilocybin Mushroom Companion* has a whole chapter devoted to trip sitting- explaining everything from how to trip sit, to how to help someone through a challenging trip – it's worth reading.

A common question I'm asked about setting is what the best setting. Only you can truly decide that, but for me personally my favorite setting is outside- – preferably a beach, but considering that I now live out in the mountains of Northern California, I can definitely say that journeying out amongst the huge trees and the mountains is just as incredible. On a small dose of around 1.2mg of psilocybin, I like to hike to take in nature and how much more alive it all appears to be, but on doses anything higher than that, I like to remain stationary during my trips – largely because it's easier to take in the experience than having to worry about maneuvering around or possibly hurting myself. Additionally, given that mushrooms come from nature itself, there's something about being outside while journeying – laying in a hammock watching the trees breathe, seeing all the colors of nature much more vividly while you are laying on a beach and playing with the sand ... these experiences are what journeying is all about to me. Just be mindful of the people you could encounter while out and about, you probably won't want to engage with strangers while you're dosing.

Journeying indoors can be just as great of an experience as well. I just encourage you to clean up your space before journeying, a cluttered environment can weigh you down while journeying. Also encouraged is to create a vibe within your trip spot. Make your spot as comfy to you as possible... have comfy pillows and blankets (sometimes your body temp can get hot/cold so having a blanket handy is nice or just comforting), diffuse some essential oils or incense, dim the lights, have a good playlist going for your trip, a journal should you want to jot down some downloads[8], some coloring books, musical instruments if you feel inclined, some juicy fruit like blueberries, mango, or grapes for an intense taste bud

---

[8] "Downloads" is often used by psychonauts or esoteric folk to describe information flowing to you from the ether or from another realm. Thoughts that seem to manifest out of nowhere.

overload sensation, or also have a blindfold on hand for moments when you want to dive deep and shut the world out. I often will wear comfortable clothing and bonus points if the clothes have trippy designs on them, which can be fun to look at when you're in the zone.

Also something to consider is to keep electronics at a minimum, at least if your goal is to take a deep dive. When I am journeying, the last thing I want to look at is any type of electronic, especially my cell phone – anytime I do catch a glimpse of it or use it, there's a weird feeling of disconnection and the technology feels so foreign to me… I tend to feel like a monkey who's discovered technology for the first time, with a rudimentary understanding of it all. Sometimes movies can be fun to watch, but as I mentioned in my introduction, movies can also be weird at times too… you never know if the characters might begin to talk about you.

Chapter 5:

Dosing

Proper dosing is something that definitely needs to be considered. Many "bad trips" are sheerly because not only was the person not in the right set or setting but they dosed with too much mushroom. My goal is to help you to avoid that so that you can go into your journey more confident that you will have a good experience.

An important tool to have available if you're working directly with mushrooms themselves and not with just capsules or magic mushroom chocolates, is a kitchen scale. Weighing out the proper dose so you know how much you're actually taking is smart to do. When you weigh out your dose, it acts as a good reference point going forward. Was that dose just perfect for you? Awesome, now you know the next time around how much to take again to try to recreate that experience (although NO two trips are exactly the same). Was the experience too much for you? Okay, well at least you know that in the future you may want to do less. Having a scale helps you to find your Goldilocks amount.

I normally consume mushrooms in the form of capsules, chocolates, or dried mushrooms (as mushroom tea). You can consume fresh mushrooms, but take note that whenever I, or pretty much anyone, mentions the amount of mushrooms they took, they're speaking about the dried weight of them. If you want to weigh out your fresh mushrooms, take into consideration that every 10 grams wet is roughly equal to 1 gram dry.

If you're someone who's new to mushrooms, or have taken a long hiatus from your last journey, my best suggestion is to start small and work up to larger doses incrementally- that is, if you're looking to dose with a large amount. Starting small helps to ease you into it and gives you a good idea what to expect. Most people I know who are considering dosing, have a lot of apprehension (thanks DARE), so starting with a small dose to get your feet wet is the right path to take. Otherwise you could overdo it, which could leave you with a really bad experience, never wanting to do mushrooms again.

So what is the right dose? That all depends on what it is you're looking for. Are you looking to microdose or macrodose?

Microdosing (.05g-.5g of dried mushrooms) is probably what has turned you onto the idea of taking mushrooms, as it's what is most commonly talked about in the media at this time. Microdosing is when you take such a small amount of mushrooms that you will likely not feel the psychoactive effects of them. With a micro amount of mushrooms you ought to feel an alleviation of stress, anxiety, or any symptoms of depression, while still leaving you with the ability to function and work if necessary. It helps turn on the creative juices, and as one of my friends who is a mother and is experienced with mushrooms mentioned, when she microdoses she's much more able to get down on her kids level and fully emerge herself in play mode, it makes her a much more in tune mother. It's important to note here that while this friend of mine is very familiar with psilocybin and its effect on her, she only microdoses and never macrodoses, while her kids are with her.

I often get asked what a good microdosing schedule is. Depending upon who you talk to, chances are you will get a different answer from each person. I don't adhere to a strict regimented schedule. I personally take one whenever I feel is necessary- should I feel a little more down in the dumps than usual, or know that I need an attitude adjustment, I will take one. The effects from a microdose tend to last for a few days for me, leaving my mood feeling lifted enough that I won't need to take one until I feel down in the dumps again. Paul Stamets suggests microdosing 5 days in a row, then taking two days off so as to not build up a tolerance. Some others suggest 1 day on 2-3 days off.[9] It's important to experiment with the microdose schedule yourself, to see what works best for you. As always, while you're learning how your body handles microdosing, I suggest doing it on a day off.

Macrodosing (.5g and up of dried mushrooms) is anything above the psychoactive threshold. I would say around .5g- 2.5g of mushrooms is a "recreational"

---

[9] https://thethirdwave.co/microdosing-psilocybin-mushrooms-stamets-stack/

29

dose, a dose which allows you to maybe enjoy a concert on a deeper level or enjoy nature a little more intensely. Anything 2.5g and up can be a much more internal experience, something that you may want to be grounded for. Taking anything more than .5g of mushrooms could start to change the way you perceive reality. Walls or trees can breathe, your senses become much more acute, patterns can start to move around, you may see visions, go to different realms, and you may also find you temporarily have synesthesia – a phenomena in which you could see sounds, taste words, or hear colors. You typically won't see things that aren't there, you'll just see things in a much more colorful, elaborate way. Emotionally, you can have moments of catharsis- purging of deep rooted emotions like fear that can leave one feeling restored. Often many will say that taking a macro dose helped them to see their own blind spots– how and why they were holding themselves back. On doses starting around 3g and up, some people report having an "ego death" which refers to your ego – all of your social constructs of the self, the labels you identify with, and the masks you wear as protection melting away, leaving you much more in touch with divinity, shedding off all the layers that can make us wound up, uptight, and less empathetic towards not just others but ourselves as well.

Worth mentioning is the "heroic dose" – coined by Terence McKenna, an American ethnobotanist, mystic, psychonaut, lecturer, author, and an advocate for the responsible use of naturally occurring psychedelic plants.[10] A heroic dose is taking 5g of

---

[10] https://en.wikipedia.org/wiki/Terence_McKenna

dried mushroom, alone, on an empty stomach, in complete darkness and silence. Terence believed that through taking a heroic dose, one could experience a profound visionary experience. I myself have taken 5g of mushrooms, and while I did it alone, on an empty stomach, outside, and not in silence, my experience was profound. It's something I will carry with me for the rest of my life. I had many cathartic releases and experienced an intense ego death that tore back all of my perceptions of myself and who I believed myself to be.[11]

It's important to understand as mentioned above, that one needs to experiment with these dosage recommendations. No two people are exactly the same. What might be enough of a dose to cause an ego-death in me, could be a dose that doesn't do the same for you. Always start small when dosing and take into great consideration to be careful of being overzealous with getting the show on the road – I've heard many stories of people taking mushrooms, not feeling anything within the first 30-60 minutes, so they take more, and they end up really throwing themselves into the deep end. Also take note that the more you take, the deeper the experience will be for you. Your 5g journey is going to be much different than your 2g journey.

---

[11] Check out my youtube video describing my heroic trip at https://youtu.be/c_SbLx-jpG4

<u>Remember:</u>

"You can always take more, you cannot take less".

Chapter 6:

The Day Of & The Journey Itself

So you've put enough thought and consideration into your experience, you've cleared your schedule for the day, and you're ready to go. But what should your day look like?

The first thing I would do is determine when it is I would like to dose. Both the day and the night have their own special attributes. During the day it's great to be outside in nature, but if you're going with an indoor journey it's nice to have the light from outside shining in through your windows especially during your first trip– sometimes darkness can set the tone for a more ominous trip. During the day is great because if you allot yourself enough time, you ought to be coming down with enough time that you should be able to get to bed with no problems. Night journeys are great if the thought of looking up at the stars and glancing into the great unknown gets you jazzed up. A trip can last anywhere from 4-8 hours (varying person to person and the method in which you take the mushrooms, e.g. mushroom tea tends to illicit a journey that's shorter for some people like me), so plan accordingly – especially if you have to hire a babysitter – and know that if you don't dose until 9pm at night, you're in for a long night.

Food is something to definitely consider the day of. I tend to recommend to anyone dosing that they dose 3 hours after their last *light* meal. If you're taking your mushrooms later in the day or evening, it's suitable to have a regular breakfast- maybe some oatmeal or eggs, have a light lunch of some fruit or a small salad, and then dose about 3-4 hours later. I generally like to dose during the day and find that taking my mushrooms on an empty stomach is much more preferred, with possibly munching on a few light things like fruit and nuts about 20 or so minutes after dosing. Also consider keeping some washed and ready fruit or easy to enjoy snacks on hand to munch on during the trip (although eating is the last thing I want to do while tripping) or for after. If you take your mushrooms early enough in the day, after you come down, you'll probably want to eat a full meal. It can be helpful to have something waiting for you in a crock pot to enjoy, or delivery is always an easy go-to as well.

In Chapter 4 I discussed set and setting. Be sure that your mindset is on track, you have an intention set, and you have your trip-spot picked out and set up so you can be comfortable. Should you choose to listen to music, already have your playlist ready to go. Some deep divers also like to keep an eye mask on hand so that they can listen to their music, pop their eye mask on for total darkness, and journey deep inside themselves. That's always a really incredible option, knowing that you don't have to stay committed to keeping the eye mask on and can remove it at any time.

After you have everything figured out, you've relaxed, had time to digest your food and to consider your intentions, it's time to journey.

When I journey I like to make my experience a ceremony. I often like to have my essential oil diffuser full and ready to go for at least 3 hours, do a walk through smudging[12] the house, my mushrooms, then myself, and then I sit and take a few deep cleansing breaths, focus on my intention and take my mushrooms in the form of mushroom tea, my favorite way to take them.

It's not rare to have people report that mushrooms makes them feel nauseous. In my personal experience, I have found that taking mushrooms in the form of tea, helps to not only curtail any major nausea, but also helps the onset of the mushrooms to be much quicker. Instead of a gradual build up to the trip, with the tea, once I start to feel it kick in, I've surpassed the buildup and am going into a full-on trip. Additionally with mushroom tea, I feel that the duration of the trip isn't as long either, although it's jam packed. That said, diarrhea or vomiting after taking your mushrooms is not abnormal. It's also not something to be scared of or resist either. It's been my experience, whenever I have sat in ceremony for other psychedelics, that the shamans encourage expelling waste – they look at it as a process of "getting well" instead of getting sick. Once in ceremony a shaman

---

[12] Smudging is something that has long been practiced by the indigenous peoples of America. It's a ritual of lighting resin or sacred herbs to correct the energy in a home, in an object, or even in a person.

spoke to me about diarrhea and vomiting, saying it's an act of expelling what no longer serves you. Trauma, ancestral baggage, toxins can all be expelled in this fashion, so don't hold back, let it come out.

After taking the tea, I like to head to the bathroom if need be, and then come back to my spot inside or outdoors, recline back and wait for it to kick in. Sometimes it can take 30 minutes for me to start feeling the effects (depending upon how full I am and whether I consumed it in tea form), sometimes it could take as long as 60 minutes. When it starts to kick in, you'll know. If you're macro dosing your perception of reality will start to change like how I mentioned in chapter 5. If you're micro dosing, you ought to start feeling a lightness to you and an ease of any heavy weight on your shoulders melt away.

Once I'm in full-on trip mode, my visions normally take over. It's not that I feel I am hallucinating, more so I am seeing how I feel we may have perceived things as children, more lucid, flowy, non-static and non-linear- whereas when we have grown into adulthood everything has become more linear because of our conditioning and lack of tuning into our imagination. As I mentioned earlier, things will look like they're breathing, patterns will move in peculiar ways, colors will be more vibrant- but this isn't the case for everyone. For reasons beyond me, not everyone has a visionary experience. During my journey, what often comes over me is a deep sense of empathy for others, especially those I may hold resentment towards. If out in nature, I will often cry alligator tears for my deep appreciation of the environment – which has helped me to be driven to lessen my impact on the earth, understanding that most of the material things I have been caught up in don't matter, which has contributed to a more minimalist lifestyle.

Throughout the journey, I tend to have no sense of time, mostly because I am so engaged with the experience that nothing else, none of my usual worries, concerns, or my to do list, matter. I am so fully present and aware that it helps me to understand just how detached I normally am in my everyday life, helping me to be more mindful in present moments even when I am not dosing.

During your own trip experience, you could encounter a bevy of different emotions or feelings bubbling up to the surface. Some of these emotions can turn negative if you continue down a mental spiral of focusing all your attention on these thoughts. This would be a good time to revisit your intention. These moments also make having a trip sitter valuable, as they can help hold space for you or provide you with a certain level of comfort or can help you to work through stuff that comes up. Otherwise, you may find that you have to do this on your own, like I did while having an ego death during a heroic dose (my dose was 5.55g dried mushrooms) - I kept questioning my reality, who I am outside of social media and am I actually the person I show up as in real life? I kept confronting the idea of who I am as a person and was able to work through it on my own… I can imagine if I was new to dosing, that would have been a very overwhelming experience if I let myself get taken for a ride on that thought loop for too long.

37

Should you find yourself having difficulty getting out of a negative head-space something's that can help include deep breathing exercises, smoking a strain of cannabis you're familiar with to help take the edge off, and repeating a mantra like "this too shall pass" or "I am okay." Worth noting, simply changing your room or environment can help as well. If you're indoors, try going somewhere safe outdoors, or if going outside isn't an option, go to another room in your house. Therapists and centers that administer psilocybin also keep benzodiazepines like Xanax on hand to help patients deal with anxious trips- while I tend to stray from pharmaceuticals, if you're prone to anxiety or panic attacks, I'd much rather you have a bit of Xanax or Valium to help calm you down rather nothing at all.

There are many things to experiment with while you are tripping. One of my favorites is mirror work – while for some people it can be really abnormal and maybe even frightening to watch your face morph around in a mirror – I on the other hand, like to use this time for deep therapy. I will look deep into my eyes while saying positive affirmations to myself – not that I even have to think about the things to say, more so, self-love pours out of my mouth, as I see beyond all of the cultural programming and appreciate the woman deep inside the meat vehicle. As I shared in the introduction, I also like to do this completely naked too to help get over my body hang ups, because much like while looking deep into my eyes, when I'm in full trip mode the self-love oozes out and I can't help but appreciate my meat vehicle too.

Journaling can be nice as well. You may receive downloads and ideas that you won't want to forget, so jotting those down is a great idea. I also encourage you to not get caught up in journaling, as some people will focus more on writing than just experiencing the journey itself.

While journeying, a lot of people report feeling called to their creative sides. It's not abnormal to dance, stretch your body, sing, play a musical instrument even if you're not musically inclined, draw, color... you name it, do anything you may feel called to do.

You may also feel sexually inclined. Whether enjoying some solo time or some time with a consenting partner, it can be an otherworldly experience. Not all people feel sexually charged while tripping, but should it happen, embrace it. If you were patterned with shame around sex or self-pleasure, this can be a good time to break down those walls and reform new healthy ideas around sex.

During your trip, listen to your body as you may feel thirsty or hungry. As mentioned earlier in the chapter, it's nice to have some fresh juicy fruit around as it feels like a bunch of lawn gnomes are doing a jig all over your taste buds when you indulge while in the zone. I just thoroughly recommend not getting into making anything you might have to prepare while you're tripping, maybe during your comedown, but not while you're in the trenches. I'd hate for you to get caught up and leave something on your stove to burn.

Speaking of your comedown, after 5 hours or so (I'll say it once again, we are all different so your experience may be shorter or longer depending on your constitution) you ought to start coming down from your experience. The come down is usually a time when you just want to relax, cuddle up, and will probably find yourself reaching for something tasty. I've also found that smoking cannabis helps to ease the comedown.

Something also worth addressing is the mushroom aftermath. I used to firmly believe that having a hangover from mushrooms was impossible. That is, until I did over 5g. The next day after taking such a large dose, I felt a little foggy in my head and lethargic. It was nothing like a hangover from alcohol, I think my system was just taxed and needed a day to recoup. I was still able to take my dogs for a walk and function as a human being, I just needed to give myself time to rest a little more and take in more water. Being mindful to nourish my body with something grounding, yummy, and healthy post journey is also crucial. Some grounding foods I enjoy post trip include ethically sourced animal protein, or foods that grow from the ground like potatoes, squash, beets, and greens.

Chapter 7:

Integration

As I share in my YouTube video titled Why Ayahuasca and Mushrooms Won't Save You13, mushrooms and ayahuasca are not an absolute cure for what is ailing you. You don't just take these things and magically your entire life will change for the better. There's more to it than that.

Enter, integration. Integration is essentially the idea of taking what you learned through your journey and finding a way to incorporate your epiphanies and learnings into your life. Yes, there are people who do mushrooms and stop drinking or smoking cigarettes after years of addiction, but for a majority of people you will find that you need to take what you have learned and find ways to weave it into your life to create lasting change.

Integration is the most important aspect of your journey, maybe even more important than the journey itself. Some people can come from a journey and feel very detached, almost like they have no idea where to start or how to carry on with their lives. Sometimes

---

[13] To watch my video Why Ayahuasca and Mushrooms Won't Save You go to https://youtu.be/eoKJAXEAZPs

these people can feel entirely uprooted and have a hard time figuring out life going forward. That's why it's so important to make mindful integration something you act upon once your journey is over to help ground you back to reality and weave what you learned into your life.

Integration can take on various forms but for most people it often looks like having a support system you can talk to to discuss your journey with. A support system can help you to unload all that you processed or all that came up for you. Having a therapist who is open to psychedelic use is a great way to unload your journey. Should a therapist not be an option for you, hop on MeetUp.com or Facebook to see if there are any psychedelic meetup groups. These psychedelic meetups are largely made up of avid and seasoned psychonauts who like to come together to discuss journeying and to help newbies make sense of their journey. It can be a great way to connect with like-minded people, who truly get what it is you just went through and can help to guide you through future experiences, too. Also just as important can be internet forums or groups on psychedelics. They may not be the same as meeting up with people in person, but to even have a group of people online to bounce your journey off of and to get support for is not to be underrated. Erowid.org

Additionally, after journeying integration can look like evaluating your current environment to see what does and what does not serve you any longer. For instance, if you're someone who has battled addiction and your psychedelic journey helped to unveil the reasons why you are addicted and you feel no longer tethered to your addiction, it's important to evaluate your circle of friends and influence. It's been my observation and experience that you are the sum of the 5 people you surround yourself with the most. If your circle includes addicts, people stuck in a rut, and those that have no desire for personal betterment, it's probably a good idea to start seeking out a new circle. Psychedelic meetups would be a great place to start to find new like-minded people for new friends. Likewise, if you discovered through your journeying that the reason why you feel so depressed is because you're working a career that doesn't bring joy or passion to your life, it's important to start figuring out next steps for stepping into a career that motivates you. Just experiencing the mushrooms will not save you, it's going to take deliberate action to ensure you keep growing and evolving long after your mushroom journey.

Chapter 8:

Conclusion

Psychedelic mushrooms are absolutely life changing in my opinion. Now, more than ever, I feel we are being called to take them to help redirect ourselves onto a path that's more harmonious with nature and the earth. As we face the consequences of our misuse of the earth's precious natural resources and the way we have exploited resources, I feel this psychedelic renaissance may be just what we need to see the error of our ways and course correct just in the nick of time.

It's my belief that mushrooms are super grounding, helping us to become less distraught and in a constant state of fight or flight while we become more grounded and centered. With an uncertain future thanks to everything surrounding Covid-19, I believe responsible mushroom use just might help pull us out of a frantic response by helping to equip us with a more grounded approach to how to prevent catastrophes like this from happening in the future, or at the very least, how to be well prepared for them or how to safely, rationally reduce their impact.

I appreciate you for being as open minded as you are to have even entertained the idea of mushrooms and the responsible use of them enough that you decided to read this book. After years of programming about how bad mushrooms are, it's awesome to see that you are willing to rewrite that programming by discovering the truth for yourself.

As you journey forward, I hope you do your due diligence to research more, soaking up as much information as necessary for you to make informed decisions going forward. I wish for you the most life changing experience possible, one that not only helps to change the trajectory of your life for the better, but one that also helps change the trajectory of the world.

Thank you for existing.
Thank you for being you.
Safe travels.

Bonus Recipe

As I have mentioned, taking my dried mushrooms in tea form is my favorite way to dose. It makes the taste more palatable, helps to reduce nausea, makes the mushrooms come on quicker, and reduces the duration of the trip.

Here is my go to for dosing with mushroom tea.

Ingredients:
- Dried psilocybin mushrooms
- Your favorite, yummy tea of choice. I enjoy Organic India's Tulsi Sweet Rose[14].
- Juice of 1/2 a lemon
- Sweetener of choice (I prefer raw, local honey)
- 6-8oz water

Instructions:
1. Weigh out your dried mushroom material and grind into a powder either with a food processor, a coffee grinder, or a blender.
2. Bring water to a boil in a kettle.
3. Add the tea bag, lemon juice, sweetener, and powdered mushrooms to a coffee cup.

---

[14] Find Organic India's Tulsi Sweet Rose here: https://amzn.to/33SRNnG

4. Pour boiling water over top and let steep for 15 minutes.
5. Option to filter out the mushrooms before consuming.
6. I typically will not consume them and don't feel it makes my experience any less potent or magical by not consuming the fungi material.

Printed in Great Britain
by Amazon

37846429R00030